Materials

KINGFISHER

Published in 2012 by Kingfisher
This edition published in 2013 by Kingfisher
an imprint of Macmillan Children's Books
a division of Macmillan Publishers Limited
20 New Wharf Road, London N1 9RR
Basingstoke and Oxford
Associated companies throughout the world
www.panmacmillan.com

ISBN 978-0-7534-3728-5

First published as *Kingfisher Young Knowledge: Materials* in 2005
Additional material produced for Macmillan Children's Books by Discovery Books Ltd

1 3 5 7 9 8 6 4 2
1SPL/0713/WKT/UTD/128MA

A CIP catalogue record for this book is available from the British Library.

Printed in China

Note to readers: the website addresses listed in this book are correct at the time of going to print.
However, due to the ever-changing nature of the internet, website addresses and content can
change. Websites can contain links that are unsuitable for children. The publisher cannot be held
responsible for changes in website addresses or content, or for information obtained through
a third party. We strongly advise that internet searches be supervised by an adult.

Acknowledgements
The publisher would like to thank the following for permission to reproduce their material. Every care has been
taken to trace copyright holders. However, if there have been unintentional omissions or failure to trace copyright
holders, we apologise and will, if informed, endeavour to make corrections in any future edition.
b = bottom, *c* = centre, *l* = left, *t* = top, *r* = right

Photographs: *cover* Shutterstock/MarcelClemens; Shutterstock/Angel Simon; Shutterstock/HomeStudio;
Shutterstock/Richard Peterson; Shutterstock/Felix Mizioznikov; *pages* 1 Getty Imagebank; 2–3 Alamy/Creatas;
4–5 Alamy/Greg Wright; 6–7 Getty Taxi; 8*bl* Corbis; 9*cl* Getty Photodisc; 9*tr* Getty Imagebank; 9*br* Getty
Imagebank; 10*l* Getty Rubberball; 10–11 Getty Stone; 11*tr* Getty Brand X; 12*bl* Science Photo Library/Colin
Cuthbert; 12*r* Alamy/Denis Hallinan; 13*t* Getty Stone; 13*b* Alamy/Sally Greenhill; 14–15 Corbis/Ron Watts;
14*b* Corbis/Lester Lefkowitz; 15*b* Getty Imagebank; 16*c* Corbis/Gary Braasch; 16*b* Getty Imagebank;
17 Corbis/Thomas Hartwell; 18*b* Corbis/David Samuel Robbins; 19*t* Photonica; 19*br* Alamy/Panorama Stock;
20–21 Getty Imagebank; 20*b* Getty Lonely Planet; 21*tl* Getty Brand X; 21*br* Rex Features; 22*b* Corbis/James
Marshall; 23*t* Getty Photodisc; 23*b* NASA; 24 Corbis/Joel W. Rogers; 25*t* Getty Imagebank; 25*bl* Getty Brand X;
26 Getty Stone; 27*tl* Alamy/Troy and Mary Parlee; 27*br* Rex Features; 28*cr* Getty Stone; 28*bl* Corbis/Owen Franken;
29*tl* Alamy; 29*b* Corbis/Charles O'Rear; 30*c* Corbis/David H. Seawell; 30–31*b* Corbis/Patrik Giardino; 31*tr* Corbis;
31*br* Alamy/D. Hurst; 32–33*t* Corbis/Richard Hamilton Smith; 32*bl* Getty Imagebank; 32*br* Corbis/Wolfgang
Kaehler; 33*l* Getty Imagebank; 33*br* Corbis/Ariel Skelley; 34*bl* Science Photo Library/Paul Whitehill; 34*c* Science
Photo Library/Eye of Science; 35*tl* Corbis; 35*b* Corbis/Jim Cummins; 36*bl* Science Photo Library/Geoff
Tompkinson; 37*tl* Corbis; 38 Getty Imagebank; 38*b* Corbis/Wolfgang Kaehler; 39*tl* Alamy/Dex Image; 39 Corbis/Ariel Skelley;
40*b* Getty Imagebank; 40*r* Getty Imagebank; 41*tl* Alamy/James Frank; 41*r* Getty Imagebank; 48 Alamy/Tim
Brightmore; 48*t* Shutterstock Images/Gary Andrews; 48*b* Shutterstock Images/Charles Taylor; 49*t* Shutterstock
Images/Michal Baranski; 49*r* Shutterstock Images/Svetlana Lukienko; 52 Shutterstock Images/Michaela Stejskalova;
53*t* Shutterstock Images/Anton V Pavlov; 53*b* Shutterstock Images/Elnur; 56 Shutterstock Images/RTimages

Commissioned photography on pages 42–47 by Andy Crawford
Thank you to models Hayley Sapsford, Cameron Green and Joley Theodoulou

Materials

Clive Gifford

KINGFISHER

Contents

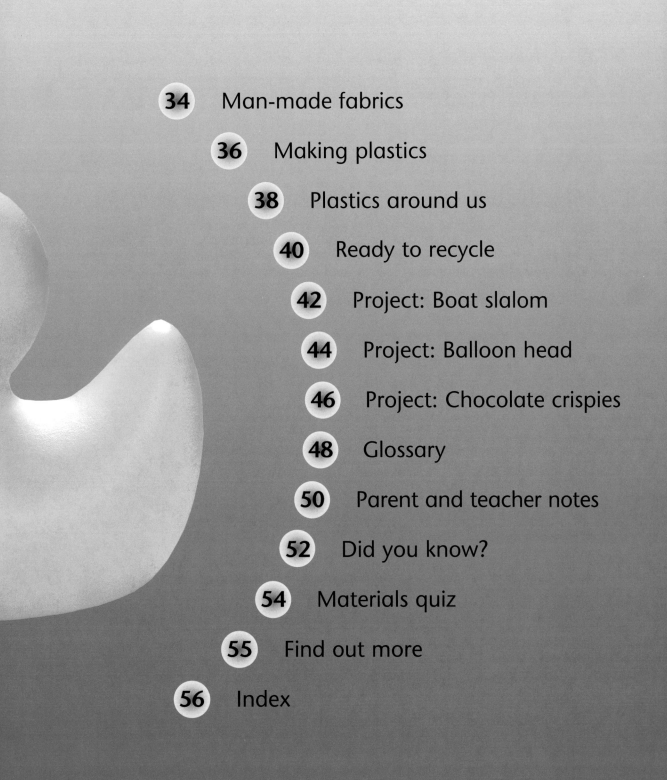

What are materials?

Materials are all around us. They are the objects that make up the world we live in. Some materials, such as rocks, are natural. Others, for example plastic and glass, are made by people.

Using materials

People use materials all the time. This picture shows many different sorts. There are liquid paints, plastic paint bottles and rollers, which are all man-made. There are also wooden shelves and a table, paper and cotton clothing. These are made from natural materials.

Liquids and solids

Liquids are wet and can flow easily.
Solid materials cannot flow, and
have a definite shape. Heat turns
some solids into liquids.

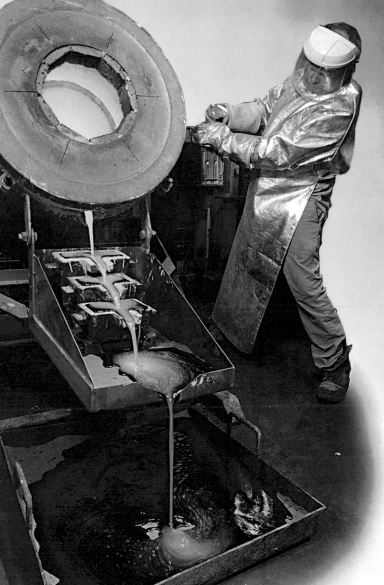

Shaping shoes

Solid iron is heated to
make it soft and easy to
shape into a horseshoe.

Liquid gold

When gold is heated,
it becomes a red, hot
liquid, which can be
poured and shaped.

Hot chocolate ice

Ice cream can be dipped into warm, melted chocolate. Once cool, the chocolate goes hard, and becomes a tasty treat.

Candlelight

A hot flame melts wax, which then runs down a candle. When the wax cools, it solidifies.

Melting lolly

In hot weather, you have to eat an ice lolly quickly before it melts. This is because the solid ice becomes watery when the sun warms it.

Floating and sinking

Some materials are very light and can float on water, or even in the air. Other materials, such as rock, are much heavier and normally sink.

Up, up and away

Helium is a gas that is lighter than air. Balloons can be filled with helium to make them float in the air.

Sinking like a stone

Many materials, such as stones, are too heavy to float in water. This means they sink to the bottom if they are thrown into a river or the sea.

Floating fun

Both this raft and the children's lifejackets are made of rubber. They float on water when filled with air. This means they are great to play with in the sea – and keep you safe too!

Stretchy and bendy

If you stretch or bend some materials, they return to their normal shape once you let go. Other materials stay in the shape you pull them.

Boing! Boing!

A spring is made of coiled wire. It jumps back to its usual shape after it has been squashed or pulled. That is why a pogo stick lets you bounce up and down.

High flyer

Vaulting poles are very flexible and can bend a long way. They help athletes to fly high up into the air.

Stretchy hairbands

Hairbands are often made of elastic. They stretch as they tie up long hair. Then they return to their normal shape and keep a perfect ponytail in place.

14 Rocky world

Rocks make up the Earth's crust. They are ancient materials and some are more than 4 billion years old. Rocks such as chalk are crumbly and soft, while others, like granite, are hard and tough.

Hot rocks

Burning hot lava comes from inside the Earth. It is runny rock, which turns hard as it cools.

Layer upon layer

Some rocks lie in layers, called strata. Over millions of years, the layers can become bent, just like the sandstone in the picture.

Wear and tear

Cold, heat, water and wind all wear away rocks little by little. Over time, amazing shapes, such as these arches, can form.

Building blocks

Rock is a very useful material that is strong, tough and hard-wearing. It can be crushed up or used in big chunks to make buildings, roads and statues, for example.

Mining for marble

Rock is mined in a quarry. Here, marble is being dug up. Marble is a hard rock that can be polished and used for floors and statues.

Big chunks

For centuries, rocks have been used to build walls. Giant blocks make up this old wall in Peru – they must have been very difficult to put in place.

Sparkling jewels

All rocks are made from minerals. Some minerals form beautiful and precious gemstones, such as these rubies and diamonds.

Living in the past

Rocks can be carved into sculptures which last a very long time. The Great Sphinx in Egypt was shaped from limestone rock around 4,500 years ago.

Clay and ceramics

Clay and ceramics are soft, earthy materials that are dug out of the ground. They can be shaped easily. When they are heated, they dry out and become very hard.

Round and round

Clay can be shaped on a potter's wheel, like the one below. Some clay objects dry out and harden in the sun. Others have to be fired in a hot oven called a kiln.

Perfect pools

Clay and ceramics are used to make
tiles and bricks. Tiles form a smooth,
waterproof surface that is perfect
for lining swimming pools.

Pretty paints

Clay objects can be
painted brightly.
A liquid called
a glaze is often
brushed on. This
makes the clay
waterproof.

Using glass

Glass is made mainly from sand heated to a high temperature. While hot, glass can be shaped. For example, it can be pressed into window panes or blown into bottles.

Playing marbles

Some glass is very thin and breaks easily. Thick glass is strong and great for making toy marbles.

Sealed in jars

Many foods, such as pickles, that contain liquids are kept in glass jars because they are waterproof and airtight. The food is stored for years without going off.

Glass of milk

Glass can be coloured or clear (see-through). A lot of drinking glasses are clear, so that you can keep an eye on what you are drinking.

With a huff and a puff

Glass objects can be made by glass-blowing. A blob of runny glass is put on the end of a tube. Blowing into the tube inflates the glass like a balloon. When the glass cools, it sets hard.

Mighty metals

Metals are shiny materials found in rocks in the ground. Some metals are hard and tough. Others are softer and weak. Because they can be cut and bent, metals are used to make many different things.

Feeling the heat

Cooking pans are often made from metals such as copper. Heat can go straight through the metal to cook the food.

Glittering gold

Precious metals, such as gold, are valuable to people. They can be made into jewellery or shaped into bars, called ingots, that are worth a lot of money.

Travelling light

In 2004, two robots landed on the planet Mars. Parts of the robots were made from lightweight metals. This made the journey to Mars easier.

24 Mixing metals

Two or more metals, or a metal and a non-metal, can be mixed together to form new materials called alloys. These alloys are useful as they can be light, strong and very hard-wearing.

Space Needle

The Space Needle towers over the American city of Seattle. It is made from steel, the world's most common alloy. Steel is used to make many things, from cutlery to cars.

Not worth its weight in gold

In the past, coins were made from precious metals such as silver and gold. Now, they are made from much cheaper metals, often alloys.

Bold as brass

Brass is made from mixing the metals zinc and copper. It is tough and hard, but can still be shaped easily. Many musical instruments are made from brass.

Wonderful wood

Wood is a useful natural material. It comes from trees. Each type of tree is made of a different kind of wood - some are soft and others are tough.

Collecting wood

Forest workers use cutting machines, called chainsaws, to chop down trees. The trees are then cut up into logs.

To the sawmill

Logs are carried by trucks or floated down rivers. They are taken to a place called a sawmill. There, different sizes and thicknesses of wood are cut and prepared for use.

Soft landing

Leftover pieces of wood can be cut up into wooden chips. These are very soft, so they are often used on the floors of playgrounds.

Working with wood

Woodwork has been an important trade and a popular hobby for thousands of years. Today, wood is used to make many objects, including buildings, boats and furniture.

Finely shaped

It is easy to cut and shape wood using tools. This person is working on a piece of wood with a metal tool called a chisel.

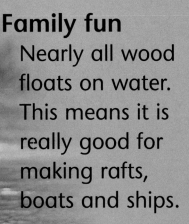

Family fun

Nearly all wood floats on water. This means it is really good for making rafts, boats and ships.

Woody pencils

Coloured pencils are made from a long stick of colour covered with a painted wooden case. Cedar wood is often used to make pencils, because it is strong.

Bright beach huts

These wooden beach huts are brightly painted. The paint helps to protect the wood from rain. If wood stays wet for a long time, it starts to go bad and can fall apart.

30 The purpose of paper

Paper is a thin, lightweight material. It can be bent and folded easily. There are a lot of different uses for paper. Most often it is used for writing or printing on.

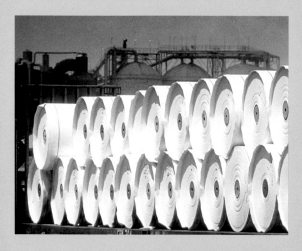

Making paper

Most paper is made in rolls in factories. It is usually produced from tiny bits of wood, but it can also be made from old paper or from rags.

Writing on paper

There are many types of writing paper. Notepaper is thin and formal writing paper is thick. Greeting cards are stiff and stand up tall. All are smooth to write on.

Daily paper

Newsprint is a special type of paper used for newspapers. It is made from ground-up wood, and is thin and cheap to produce.

Paper containers

Milk and juice cartons are made from paper. They are covered in plastic to make them waterproof. Many other papers, such as kitchen towels, soak up liquids.

Natural fabrics

Fabrics are made from long strands of material, called threads, that are woven together. Many threads come from plants and animals.

girls wearing kimonos

Smooth as silk

Silk is a beautiful fabric. It comes from thread spun by a silkworm while it is in its cocoon. It takes 3,000 cocoons to make a kimono.

Cotton buds

Cotton is a plant with big, fluffy buds, called bolls. These are collected from the fields, and washed. They are then pulled into long threads and spun into fabric.

Warm wool

Wool comes from the coats of sheep and other animals, such as some goats and camels. It can be knitted into snug clothes and blankets.

Man-made fabrics

Some fabrics are not natural, but are made from a natural raw material, such as coal. They are man-made, and are called synthetic fabrics.

Velcro hooks and loops
Velcro is made from one strip of small hooks and another strip of tiny loops. The hooks catch in the loops when the strips are pressed together.

Flying high

Nylon is a light, strong fabric. It is used not just for clothing, but also for ropes, fishing nets and even parachutes.

Synthetics in sport

Synthetic fabrics are often used to make sports clothing. This boy's shorts, vest and trainers are all made from different lightweight fabrics.

Making plastics

Plastics are always man-made. People have learned to make them out of other substances, especially oil.

Plastic penguins

When heated, plastic can be shaped easily. It can be stretched and made into tubes or sheets, or it can be poured into moulds to make objects, such as these toy penguins.

Creating cartons

To make a bottle, hot plastic is poured into a mould. A machine blows in air, which presses the plastic to the sides of the mould. The cool plastic sets in a bottle shape.

Fabulous for food

Polystyrene is plastic foam.
The foam is made by
blowing bubbles of air into
hot plastic. It keeps things
warm and is lightweight –
perfect for holding food.

Plastics around us

Plastic is used to make all sorts of objects, from furniture to paints and toys. Plastic does not rot quickly. This causes a problem with rubbish. Re-using and recycling plastic helps to cut down waste (see page 40).

Toy brickwork
Plastic bricks are hard-wearing, tough and easy to clean. Many plastics are also cheap to make.

Beach life

Plastics can be made very light in weight. Beachballs, balloons and blow-up swimming pools are all made of plastic that can be filled up with air.

Singing in the rain

Plastic sheets can be cut and glued or sewn together to make brightly coloured, waterproof clothes. This makes plastic an ideal material for raincoats, hats and wellies.

Ready to recycle

Many unwanted materials can be collected and turned into new materials. This is called recycling. Recycling helps to cut down waste.

the recycling symbol

Recycling at home

Many materials can be recycled, for example, glass, plastic and paper. This family is sorting out its recycling rubbish. Each material goes in a different container.

Fizzy drinks to fleeces

A lot of fleece jackets are made from old fizzy drink bottles. The plastic bottles are shredded and turned into thread. About 25 bottles are needed for a fleece.

Swinging time

Some items are re-used rather than recycled. This old tyre, for example, has been given a new job as a great swing.

Boat slalom

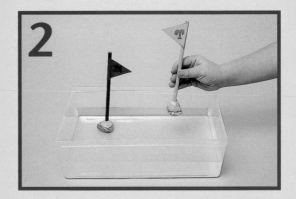

Blow a boat around a course

See how one material floats and another sinks with this fun and easy project.

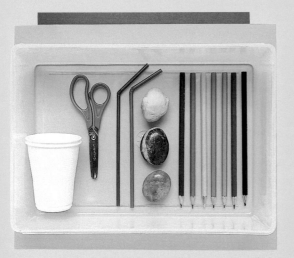

You will need
- Waterproof modelling clay
- Two stones
- Two pencils
- Two pieces of card, 3cm x 3cm x 2cm, decorated with a picture
- Glue
- Wide, shallow container
- Water
- Scissors
- Plastic cup
- Drinking straw 10cm long
- Square piece of coloured-in paper, 6cm x 6cm

1 Press modelling clay onto a stone and push a pencil into the top of it. Glue the card onto the end of the pencil as a flag. Now you have a slalom pole. Repeat.

2 Half fill the container with water and place the slalom poles in the middle of the bowl, with 10 centimetres between each. The poles should stick out of the water.

3 To make a boat, cut around a plastic cup, about 2.5 centimetres from its bottom. Stick modelling clay into the base.

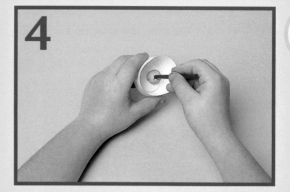

4 For the mast, push a plastic straw into the modelling clay so that it sticks straight up in the middle of the base of the cup.

Put your boat at the start of the slalom course and blow it around the poles. Take it in turns with a friend to send your boat whizzing around the course.

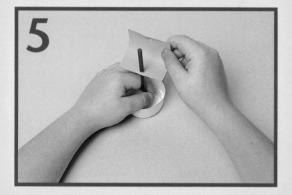

5 With scissors, make a small hole in the top and bottom of the paper. Push the paper onto the straw through the holes. You have a sailboat that will float!

Balloon head

Papier mâché model

See how you can use lots of materials to create a sculpture of a head.

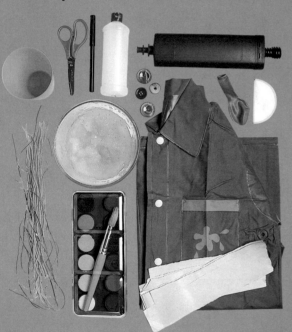

You will need

- Newspaper
- Overall (optional)
- Balloon
- Balloon pump (optional)
- Plastic cup
- Strips of thin paper
- Colour paints
- Paint brushes
- Bowl of ready-mixed wallpaper paste
- Glue
- Coloured buttons
- Wool or silvery strands
- Marker pen

1

Cover a work surface with newspaper. Blow up the balloon. Place the knotted end of the balloon in a plastic cup.

2

Take a strip of paper, cover it in paste and stick it on the balloon. Continue doing this until the balloon is covered. Leave to dry.

3

4

Repeat step 2 three more times, so that your balloon is covered in four layers of paper strips. Let the head dry fully for a day.

Now paint your balloon head in a skin colour – brown, pink or white. Make sure the whole head is covered. Let the paint dry.

5

Decorate the papier mâché balloon with wool or silvery strands for the hair, and buttons for the eyes and nose. Colour in a mouth in pen. You could use other materials, such as paper hair, for more model heads.

Chocolate crispies

A tasty chocolate treat

See how chocolate can change from a solid into a liquid, and back into a solid again.

microwave not shown

You will need

- Microwave
- Microwavable bowl
- 1 large bar (150g) of cooking chocolate
- Large spoon
- 70g rice crispies
- Small spoon
- Set of cake cases
- Plate
- Airtight container

1

Break up the bar of chocolate into single pieces and put them in the bowl. Microwave this for 90 seconds on full power.

2

Ask an adult to take the bowl out of the microwave, and stir the chocolate. If it has not all melted, heat it for another 15 seconds.

Sprinkle the rice crispies on the melted chocolate. Stir the mixture until all the crispies are coated and the chocolate is used up.

Spoon a dollop of mixture into each cake case and put on a plate to cool for an hour. Use up all of the mixture.

Once cooled and hardened, the chocolate crispies are ready to be stored in an airtight container…

…or eaten immediately!

Glossary

Air – the mixture of gases that
   we breathe
Airtight – closed to the air
Arches – curved openings in rock

Cedar – a large evergreen tree
Chips – small pieces of a material
   after it has been cut or chopped
Coal – a hard black rock found
   underground

Cocoon – a covering around an
   insect made from silky thread
Crust – the hard, rocky surface
   of the Earth
Elastic – a stretchy material
Fired – baked at a very high
   temperature
Flexible – bendy or stretchy
Flow – to run like water
Formal – proper or official
Gas – a shapeless substance,
   such as air, that is not a solid
   or a liquid
Ground-up – crushed into very
   fine pieces
Inflates – fills with gas
Iron – a strong, hard metal used
   to build or make things
Lava – melted rock on the
   Earth's surface

Lightweight – not weighing much

Limestone – a white rock that is used for building and making cement

Man-made – made by people

Mined – dug out of the ground

Minerals – natural substances in the Earth's rocks

Moulds – hollow, shaped containers

Natural – found in nature, not man-made

Oil – a thick, sticky liquid found underground

Produced – made

Raw material – material used to make other materials

Recycling – turning a material that is not needed into something that can be used again

Rot – to go bad and fall apart

Rubber – a tough, elastic material made from the milky fluid of a tropical plant

Sandstone – a rock containing tiny grains of sand tightly packed together

Shredded – cut up into very small pieces

Silkworm – a type of caterpillar

Solidifies – turns from liquid to solid

Spun – twisted quickly

Steel – a hard, strong alloy, which is made by mixing the metal iron and the chemical carbon

Substance – a material

Trade – a job or business

Valuable – worth a lot of money

This book includes material that would be particularly useful in helping to teach children aged 7–11 elements of the English and Science curricula and some cross-curricular lessons involving Geography and Art.

Extension activities

Reading
Look through the book, finding all the text that mentions food. What materials are used for storing food? What materials are used in the cooking of food?

Writing
Create a table of information showing six different materials and their key characteristics, with pictures of how they might be used.

Plan a story about a superhero made of an unusual material, such as 'Rubber Man' or 'Metal Woman'. Consider what the material is like, what it would allow them to do and if there is anything they would have to avoid.

Speaking and listening
Which material is most useful to you? Which could you live without? Prepare a two-minute talk on what you think and why.

Science
The book is about the topic of materials and rocks. It also includes links to the themes of solids, liquids and gases (pp8–9, 10, 20–21, 22, 34–35, 36–37, 39), forces (pp10–11, 12–13, 27–28, 39) and insulation (pp22, 33, 35, 37, 41).

Make a survey of all the materials in your home (you could start with one room). Think about why objects are made of that material. Organize your findings into a chart, showing the object, the material from which it is made and why it is used for that purpose.

Find five different metals and alloys in your house. Ask an adult to help you identify the various metals. Why are they used for this purpose?

Collect some rocks from your local area. Group them by colour, or by how dark or light they are, or by texture (rough or smooth?). Use a magnifying glass to study the size of the grains that form them. Write down or draw all the differences between your rocks. Can you find out what rocks you have collected?

Cross-curricular links

Art and design: Make a collage that uses as many different materials as possible, such as newspaper clippings, shopping bags, tinfoil, etc. Junk modelling is another way to re-use materials creatively.

Geography: Read pages 40–41. What could you do at home or school to re-use or recycle more of your waste? You could write a simple report, or design a poster encouraging others to act, or, best of all, start a recycling plan yourself and keep at it.

History: Choose any period in the past (such as Roman Britain, or Victorian). What materials did they not have? How did that affect their lives?

Using the projects

Children can follow or adapt these projects at home. Here are some ideas for extending them:

Pages 42–43: Experiment with different boat shapes. Can you make the boat sail faster, or stay afloat for longer? Try making boat shapes from different materials, such as tinfoil or modelling clay. Which types of boat float best?

Pages 44–45: Can you make a head that looks like you, or your favourite celebrity? Choose the best materials to make a hat for it.

Pages 46–47: Try using cornflakes instead of crispies. What other ingredients could you change or add?

- Diamonds are 90 times harder than any other natural substance found on Earth. Dentists' drills have a diamond coating.

- Gold is so soft and easily worked that you could roll 30 grams of it into a hair-thin wire 80 kilometres long!

- In 2010, a rare 25-carat pink diamond became the most expensive jewel ever sold at auction. It was bought by a British man named Laurence Graff for 29 million pounds!

- An alloy is always harder than any of the materials from which it is made.

- Make sure you recycle all the paper in your house. Every tonne of paper recycled saves 18 trees.

- There are more than 4,000 types of mineral on Earth. Scientists are discovering new minerals all the time.

- Volcanoes eject melted rock called lava. The longest flow of lava ever measured was from Laki, a volcano in southern Iceland, in 1783. The lava stretched for almost 70 kilometres!

- Glass can form naturally. When lightning strikes sand, the heat sometimes fuses the sand into long, slender glass tubes called fulgurites. Another name for them is petrified lightning.

- Hardwoods come from deciduous trees (trees that lose their leaves) and softwoods come from evergreen trees (trees that don't lose their leaves).

- The hardest wood in the world comes from the Schinopsis tree in South America. Because of its hardness, the tree is nicknamed *quebracho*, which means 'axe-breaker' in Spanish. The wood is used to construct railway sleepers.

- The coal we dig up from under the ground is formed from the remains of trees and plants that died up to 400 million years ago!

- One silkworm cocoon contains about a kilometre of silk thread. Silk originally came from China, where its source was kept a secret for hundreds of years.

- Water is the only material in nature that can be a solid, a liquid and a gas. When heated, solid ice melts into liquid water. Then it evaporates into the air as gas.

- An orange floats on water because the peel is full of trapped air pockets, making the orange light for its size. When you remove the peel, the orange weighs a lot for its size and it sinks in water.

- Wool is used in some unusual places. The covering on a tennis ball and the tip of a felt-tip pen are both made from wool.

- Nylon was discovered in 1935 and was the world's first synthetic fibre. One of its first uses was in World War II. Nylon was found to be the perfect replacement for silk in the construction of parachutes. It was just as light but stronger and far cheaper to produce.

- The most expensive oil used in perfumes is musk oil. It comes from the glands of male musk deer, which are found in the mountains of Asia. One kilogram sells for 28 thousand pounds!

- On average, 323 plastic bags are taken into our homes every year, but a bag takes 500 years to rot when it is thrown away.

Materials quiz

The answers to these questions can all be found by looking back through the book. See how many you get right. You can check your answers on page 56.

1) Which of these materials is not natural?
   A – Metal
   B – Cotton
   C – Plastic

2) Helium is...
   A – A liquid
   B – A gas
   C – A solid

3) What are layers of rock called?
   A – Strata
   B – Granite
   C – Lava

4) Which of these statements is not true?
   A – Some woods are soft while others are very tough
   B – Nearly all wood floats on water
   C – Wood is waterproof and does not rot

5) Which material goes dry and hard when it is heated?
   A – Clay
   B – Limestone
   C – Marble

6) Plastic is made from which raw material?
   A – Wood
   B – Oil
   C – Coal

7) Glass can be shaped...
   A – While it is hot
   B – While it is cool
   C – On a potter's wheel

8) Which of these is not an alloy?
   A – A mixture of two metals
   B – A mixture of two non-metals
   C – A metal and a non-metal mixed together

9) Silk is a material created by which animal?
   A – Silkworm
   B – Silkslug
   C – Silksnail

10) Which of these is not a synthetic fabric?
   A – Wool
   B – Nylon
   C – Velcro

11) Which of these objects is not elastic?
   A – A spring
   B – A candle
   C – A hairband

12) Twenty-five drinks bottles can be recycled into what?
   A – A newspaper
   B – A fleece jacket
   C – A tyre

Books to read

Changing Materials (Ways into Science) by Peter Riley, Franklin Watts, 2007

Materials (Go Facts: Physical Science) by Ian Rohr, A&C Black, 2009

Minerals, Rocks and Soil (Sci-Hi) by Barbara Davis, Raintree, 2010

Recycling Materials (Making a Difference) by Susan Barraclough, Franklin Watts, 2006

Rocks and Minerals (Basher Science) by Dan Green and Simon Basher, Kingfisher, 2009

Solids, Liquids and Gases (Material World) by Robert Snedden, Heinemann, 2008

Using Materials series (Raintree Perspectives) by Chris Oxlade, Raintree, 2005

Places to visit

Techniquest Science Centre, Cardiff
www.techniquest.org
The UK's first science centre has a huge selection of stunning and ground-breaking exhibits. Investigate different kinds of materials, from natural rocks and minerals to strange man-made substances that glow when heated.

National Glass Centre, Sunderland
www.nationalglasscentre.com
Explore how glass is produced, the history of glass making and the ways in which glass is used. You will also get to see some great glass exhibits. You can even try glass-blowing yourself and make your own items from glass.

Natural History Museum, London
www.nhm.ac.uk/nature-online/earth/rock-minerals/index.html
The museum is home to one of the largest collections of minerals in the world. It explains how some of them can be used in everyday situations. In The Vault you can see some of the most rare and precious gems, including amazing, coloured diamonds.

Australian Fossil and Mineral Museum, Bathurst, Sydney
www.somervillecollection.com.au
This museum features some of the finest and rarest examples of minerals in the world. Highlights include crystals from more than 100 mine sites in Australia and garnets that are 2,000 million years old, as well as diamonds, sapphires, rubies and emeralds.

Websites

www.bbc.co.uk/schools/ks2bitesize/science/materials
Find out about the characteristics of different materials and how materials can change.

www.woodlands-junior.kent.sch.uk/revision/Science
This site has interactive games and activities about materials.

www.recycling-guide.org.uk
Find out how you can recycle different materials at home.

Materials quiz answers

1) C
2) B
3) A
4) C
5) A
6) B
7) A
8) B
9) A
10) A
11) B
12) B